Contents

Meet the Marvels! 2

Captain Marvel Meets
the Metal Monster 8

In this comic ...

Billy

Little sis

Metal Monster

Meet the Marvels!

Billy and his little sister were normal kids.

"Look out!"

"You are so annoying, Billy!"

"Hey!"

Then they met a wizard called Shazam.

"Shout my name aloud, and you will get super powers!"

"Shazam!"

"Cool! Now we have super powers!"

Billy had lots of fun as Captain Marvel.

Hang on! We will be on the ground soon.

"All safe and sound!"

"Take us up to the clouds!"

"Again! Again!"

"Sorry! I have too many jobs to do!"

"Shazam!"

Krakout!

Billy was back to normal.

Billy was a television reporter.

Have you got any hot choc?

Morning!

Enjoy it!

I am a top reporter!

Go out and find a good story, boy!

Top reporter, hey? We will see.

Just then ...

Crash!

Kapoy!

Shatter!

Boom!

A metal monster!

You have just found a story, Billy!

Shaz ...

What, boy?

I did not say anything, sir!

See you!

Oops! I nearly let it slip!

Back at home ...

Shazam!

Krakout!

Captain Marvel Meets the Metal Monster

Crash!

Kapoy!

Bam!

A metal monster – that is different!

Smack!

Ouch!

The monster shot its stun guns.

Zap!

Buzz!

Zap!

Billy's little sis came to help.

But she was too late!

Crack!

Slam!

Oh no! He is out for the count!

Are you okay?

Look out!

Slam!

Thanks, little sis.

That was close!

Crash!

You are so brave!

Just doing my job!

Come on, little sis!

Oh no! Look!

The monster was back!

The metal monster took hold of Captain Marvel!

I will get you out!

Turn the monster off!

Found it!

Click!

13

There was a loud sound.
The metal monster blew up.

Crack-a-boom!

I am proud of you, little sis!

Hooray!

Thank you, Captain Marvel!

Any time! Just doing my job!